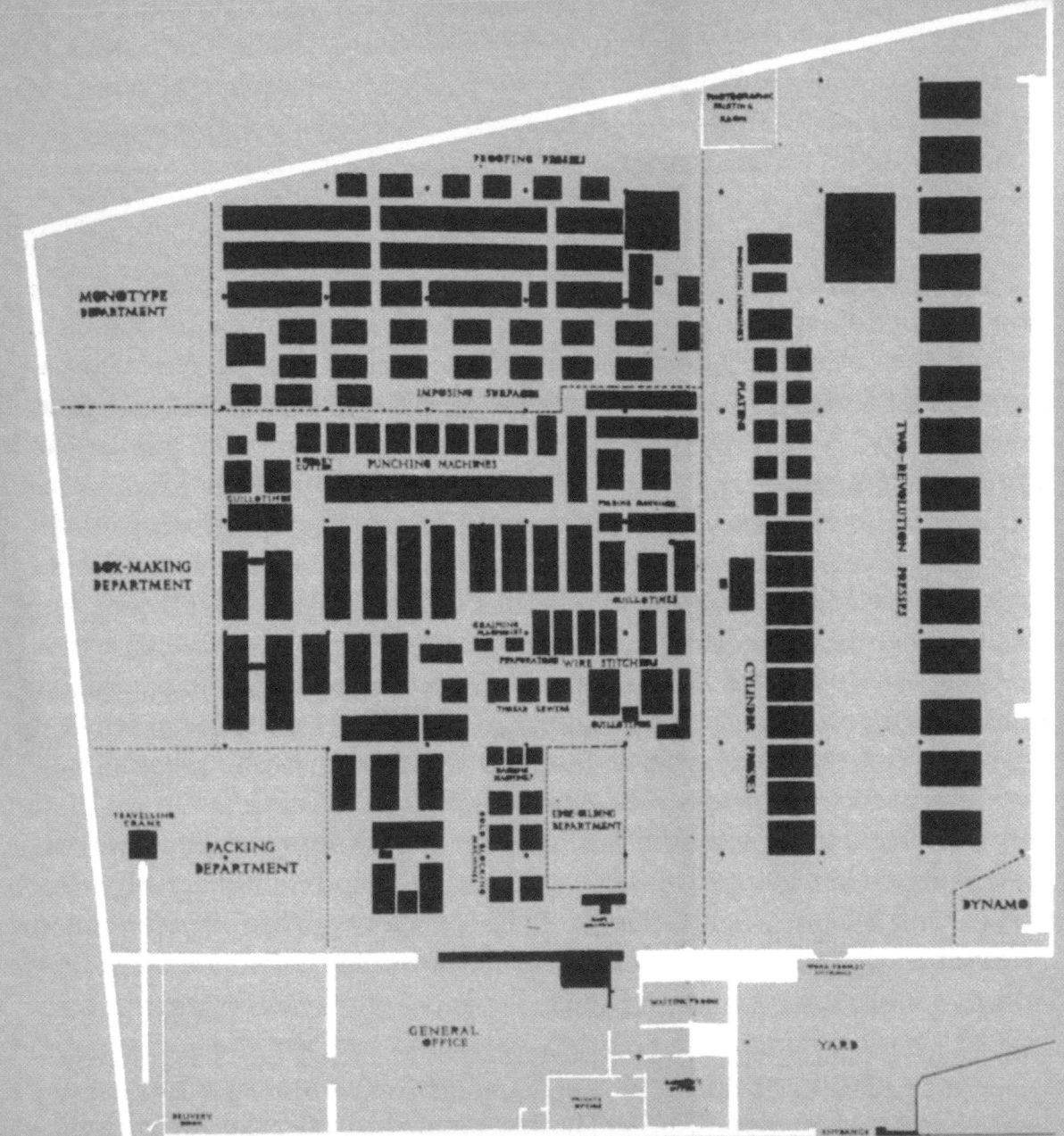

Ruth Artmonsky

A PIONEERING PRINTER

Lund Humphries of Bradford

A Pioneering Printer
Lund Humphries of Bradford

Published by Artmonsky Arts
Flat 1, 27 Henrietta Street
London WC2E 8NA
Telephone: 020 7240 8774
Email: artmonskyruth@gmail.com

Text © Ruth Artmonsky 2022

The Jacket of this book is based on the invitation to an exhibition celebrating the 55th anniversary of Lund Humphries, 1939

The illustration opposite the title page shows a plan if the Lund Humphries works, c.1960

The monogram at the foot of the title page is reproduced from the Lund Humphries type specimen book; *Book Types*. It is also illustrated in the 1926 edition of *Monotype Recorder* – printed by Percy Lund Humphries

ISBN 978-1-9163845-5-2

Designed by Webb & Webb Design Limited
www.webbandwebb.co.uk

Printed in Great Britain

Contents

Foreword — 7

Percy Lund and Edward Walter Humphries — 9

The Bradford works — 17

Eric Beresford Humphries and Eric Craven Gregory — 25

The London base — 33

Penrose Annual — 39

The Bedford Square exhibitions — 47

Herbert Spencer and Typographica — 59

Art book publishing — 67

A jobbing printer to the end — 73

Appendices — 82

Dedicated to
Charles Lubelski,
for his generosity in letting me snitch tidbits from his extremely will researched book on Lund Humphries:
Passion, Pride and Printing.

Foreword

Ruth Artmonsky

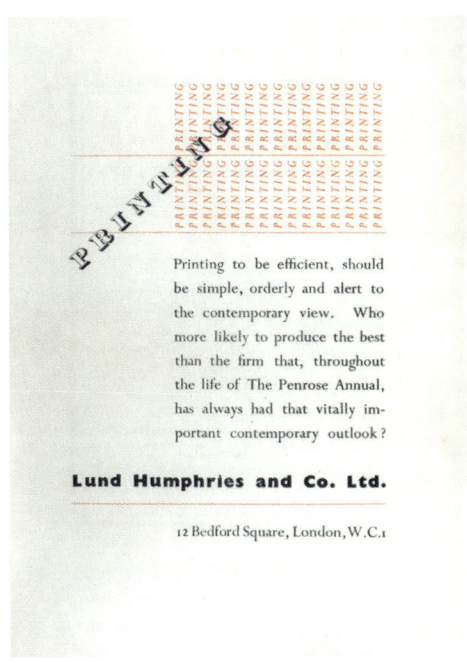

Above A 1937 Lund Humphries advertisement in the Penrose Annual.

Some years ago, on a whim, I brought myself some two dozen or so Penrose Annuals, at one time one of the leading journals on printing and the graphic arts. I wanted them for the sheer joy of idly turning the pages, stopping where I would, and learning, learning, learning.

I had already written small essays on several of the British inter-war printers as Cowell's of Ipswich, Vincent Brooks, Day & Sons and the Baynard Press, and wondered why no one had thought the proprietor and printer of the *Penrose Annual*, Lund Humphries, sufficiently distinguished to have a volume devoted to it.

I rang the then proprietor to inquire about archives; whoever answered the phone assured me that they had been disposed of. Absorbed, as I was, with other titles at the time I let the matter rest.

However, the idea intermittently returned and, having recently written on Peter Gregory (a one time Chairman of the Lund Humphries) and on Edward McKnight Kauffer (a one time Design Director for the company), I decided to gather together what notes I had made over the years, and, using my own design library as my resource, (now being unable to visit archives), I decided to weave together, as well as I could, a tribute to this exceptional firm, based in Bradford, that, for much of the 20th century, was one of a handful of printers-cum-publishers who combined technical progressiveness with contemporary aesthetics.

Photography for Novices

The Primus Handbook

4th Edition.

Price 1/- nett.

Percy Lund and Edward Walter Humphries

Percy Lund (1864-1943) and Eric Humphries (1864-1948), born in the same year, some two hundred miles away from each other, in Bradford and Wooton Bassett respectively, were to become the oddly assorted pair who converted a Bradford printer, that was, for a time, as well known as a photographic equipment manufacturer and retailer as a press, into one of the most progressive printing and art book publishing companies in Britain, with an international reputation. Dissimilar in personality and in interests, they appear to have been sufficiently complementary in what they could offer in management, to make their pairing work.

Bradford, at the time, was no provincial backwater, but had morphed from being a small settlement in the foothills of the Pennines into a metropolitan borough (awarded 1847), and then into a city in 1897. With natural resources of coal and water it had developed as a textile town, growing from what was originally a cottage industry into one of some hundred mills, with the reputation of being 'the wool centre of the world'.

A visitor, then, might possibly have described it as dirty, polluted and disease ridden; but, on the other side of the industrialised coin, as it were, it could be seen to have Victorian grandeur – striking civic buildings and parks, advanced educational institutions, and considerable cultural activity, much of this emanating from the patronage of wealthy

Above Percy Lund & Co first logo, boy climbing pear tree.
Opposite 4th edition of *Photography for Novices*, The Primus Handbook.

mill-owning families as the Listers. It was the Listers who funded an art gallery and had a park named after them, and the Rutherstons who actively supported the Bradford Arts Club; and, for the betterment of the education of its populous, there was a grammar school, a technical college, an art school, a free library and a Mechanics' Institute; all of this along with a myriad of voluntary societies furthering interests from science and nature to theosophy and temperance. Bradford was a city epitomising Victorian enterprise, crusading, and civic pride.

All this bustle, energy and enthusiasm meant work for printers – from the need for common or garden labels, ledgers and advertising, to exhibition catalogues and concert programmes. The demand was such that it has been estimated that, at the turn of the century, there were some seventy presses in Bradford and its outlying area, most generalists, but some specializing, for example, in packaging or in magazine publishing.

Percy was brought up in Ilkley and there joined his father's flourishing printing and stationary business. It had just acquired the local newspaper – the Ilkley Free Press – when his father suddenly died. This seems to have given Percy the freedom to do things his own way, and soon the newspaper was sold off, and the company moved, lock, stock, and barrel to the centre of Bradford, to the hub of commercial activity, where opportunities beckoned.

Although Percy was not disinterested in the printing side of the business, his passion, from adolescence, was for photography. Still in his teens he had become a member of the Leeds Naturalist Club and made a short-lived attempt, with friends, to run a photographic magazine – *The Practical Naturalist*. As an active, outdoor, person he combined his enthusiasm for rambling, cycling, potholing, and the like, with his photographic interests, carrying with him a camera

Above Percy Lund 1864 -1943.

Opposite Left Cover for the Bradford Philharmonic Sunday Concerts 1928 -1929 season, held at the Theatre Royal, Bradford. *Right* Souvenir programme for the Third Birthday Party, 1928 -1929 season. Cover designs by E McKnight Kauffer.

and honing his photographic know-how and skills.

At the age of twenty he established his own business – Percy Lund & Co. – which, by the time he moved it into Bradford, was not only offering printing services, but selling photographic equipment and materials. Soon it was to start to publish books and magazines on photography, publications, aimed at both amateur and professional photographers. He issued a monthly 'trade' magazine – The Photographer's World, and, for the amateur, The Practical Photographer. In addition he started to publish a series of books Lund's Library of Photography and occasionally wrote one himself. Many of these publications contained his own photographs as well as articles written by him.

Photography was to dominate even the printing side of the business, as in an early advertisement –

'...offer the resources of their Establishment to Photographers and Photographic Material Dealers requiring any kind of printing from a handbill or circular to a catalogue of many pages.'

By 1890 Percy Lund & Co. could be described as printer, publisher, photographic materials manufacturer, merchant and magazine proprietor. In all this flurry of activity Percy did not think small or local, and soon his books and publications were being distributed internationally through overseas agents.

Although all of this activity must have given Percy considerable satisfaction, and was profitable, it could be described as something of an ego-trip, for his uncle Charles (his father's brother and business partner, who was keeping an accountancy eye on Percy Lund & Co.) appears

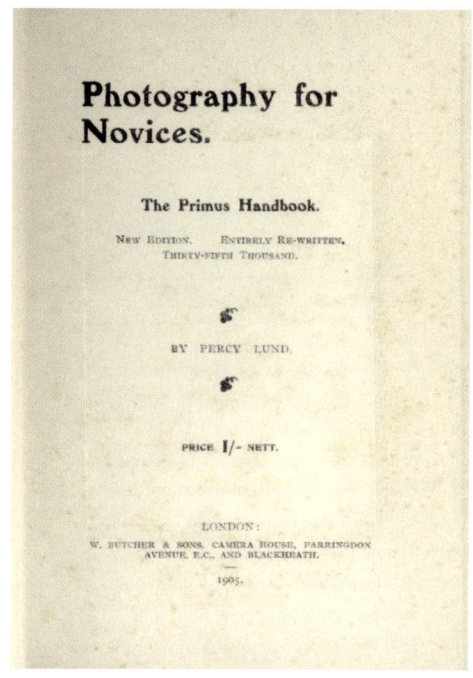

Above The Primus Handbook, Photography for Novices, 4th Edition, Entirely Rewritten, by Percy Lund. Published by W. Butcher & Sons, 1905.

Percy Lund and Edward Walter Humphries

to have had some concern as to the direction the company was taking, thinking it might benefit from a steadying hand. In 1895 he wrote a letter to Edward Walter Humphries, a young man working in Norwich at the time, inviting him to join Percy's enterprise –

> *'…my nephew Percy Lund. He has a large concern here in Bradford which we think is too heavy for one pair of shoulders and his family have been urging him for some time past to try and get a suitable person to join him.'*

And 'suitable' Humphries proved to be. Educated in York, he had joined Jarrold's of Norwich, which had both a printing and publishing business, along with a department store and retail outlets. Although it is not recorded as to whether Humphries had done a full printing apprenticeship or not, it is thought that his position as a retail manager with the firm would have made him generally familiar with most aspects of the business. It is not known for sure how Uncle Charles had come across Humphries but one suggestion is that he had known Humphries' aunt, who was headmistress of a Bradford girls' school.

In 1895 Humphries became Percy's partner and the firm became Percy Lund, Humphries & Co. The photography activities rapidly disappeared and the company began to focus its efforts on its printing side. Yet, paradoxically, it was its printing of a photographic company's catalogue that resulted in Percy Lund, Humphries & Co. becoming both proprietor and printer of *The Penrose Annual*, a major publication appealing to both the printing industry and graphic designers world wide – a publication that was to enhance the reputation of Lund Humphries throughout most of the company's existence.

Although Percy is described as keeping watch on the Bradford

Above Edward Walter Humphries 1864 -1948.

site whilst Humphries made marauding visits to London, where the company now had an office, to pick up plum commissions, Humphries must have immersed himself in the technical aspects of printing for later he was to hold key post in the printing industry at a local and national level, in sequence – Chairman of the Bradford Master Printers' Association, President of the Yorkshire Master Printers' Alliance and, by 1920, President of the National Federation of Master Printers. And, in addition, Humphries was to become a Freemason, a Governor of Bradford Grammar School and President of Bradford's Rotary Club – a worthy citizen.

Percy, on the other hand, became President of Bradford's Photographic Society, President of the Yorkshire Photographic Union, along with more esoteric roles as President of the Bradford Theosophical Society, although he too appears to have been a Freemason. Anthony Bell, a future Director of Lund Humphries, supplies a charming picture of Percy –

'a very decent man – straight-in-the-eye, erect, Norfolk jacketed and with a glint of humour and humanity very apparent. Utterly lacking in self-importance.'

Although there is not a parallel description of Humphries, it is suggested that the adjectives 'responsible', 'solid', and 'conventional' might apply. Percy comes across as the unconventional energetic enthusiast, Humphries as the grounded businessman. Whatever their differences, the two worked as joint Managing Directors (Percy in the additional role of Chairman), building up Lund Humphries to be an exceptionally high quality printers. They were to be succeeded by Edward's son Eric and by another Bradford man, 'Peter' Gregory, Percy having no children or, apparently, suitable heirs.

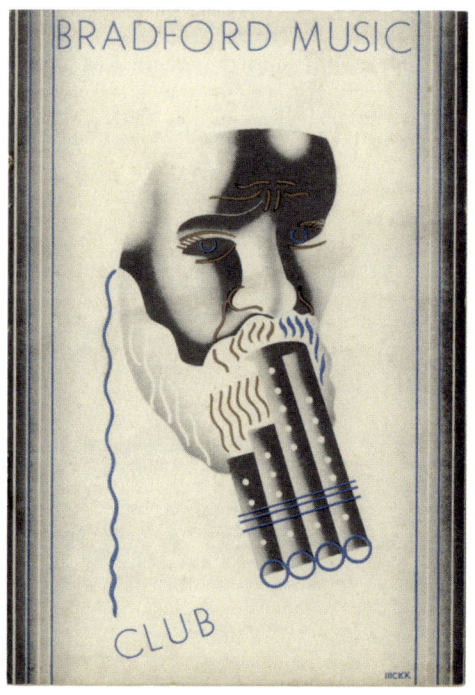

Above *Bradford Music Club*, concert programme, The Midland Hotel, Bradford, 1937. Eric C. Gregory was the Hon. Treasurer of the club.

Opposite Loading one of the company's horse drawn wagons.

The Bradford works

'The first thing that struck me was the magnificent old mill chimney that dominates the attractive jumble of textile buildings into which the equipment of a modern printing press is improbably but comfortably laid out.'
Nicolas Barker, Head of Conservation at the British Library, 1960s

It would seem no coincidence that, on the sudden death of his father, Percy Lund cleared the stable, as it were, sold off his newspaper, and relocated his company to Bradford. As Barker wrote, Percy Lund Humphries Ltd. was eventually to occupy a disused textile mill and was to remain on the site, adding accretions from time to time. Barker describes the result as 'comfortable', but others have questioned whether, in the long run, it was to prove less efficient than starting from scratch with a purpose-built works.

Initially, because of Percy's obsession with all things photographic, the ground floor of the works was allocated to deal with that side of his business, the first floor holding the printing machinery, the second, the composing room.

Although the building might have been old, as Barker wrote, its contents were 'modern', for throughout its existence Lund Humphries

Above Right The works, 1907.
Opposite Proofing in the composing room c.1910.

sought the latest and most efficient machinery, equipment and type, and was ahead of much of the field in this. An 1893 survey of Yorkshire industries noted of the company –

> 'The general printing and manufacturing stationery section is as ably and successfully coordinated as that devoted to photography; the careful and artistic workmanship in this department has been frequently and eulogistically noticed by the journals of the printing trade...'

Whilst using some locally manufactured machinery, such as the Wharfedale flat-bed letter press machine, which had the advantage of local maintenance facilities, the Works imported a Miele press from Chicago and, in 1904, was one of the earliest printers to install the Lanston Monotype composing system. The Penrose Annual of the year, championing the event, wrote

> '...the very wonderful machine which has made it possible to dispense with the old laborious and tedious way of picking up type letter by letter by the deft fingers of the compositor.'

The system consisted of two machines – one to punch letters on to a paper spool, the other to read the spool and then cast lines of type in molten metal.

The adjectives 'first' and 'foremost', as attributes to the Works, tumble out, one after the other – one of the first to have its own studio (employing the young Frank Newbould, just out of Bradford art school, who was to become a leading poster designer); one of the earliest to build up a lithography department; an early owner of its own delivery

Above Section of the binding department, c.1910.

Above Press room, 1907.

Below Monotype keyboard room, 1907.

vans, and so on. This continual up-dating went on through to the 1950s and 60s when, after a review of all the Press' machinery at the end of the war, it set up its own laboratory, a rare if not unique event, albeit employing a woman scientist – Margaret Barraclough – was probably a first for the industry. And, perhaps rather late in the day, it had actually built a new administration block, yet again showing its progressiveness by commissioning a mural from the pop-artist Eduardo Paolozzi.

And along with all its technical efficiency, a major strength of Lund Humphries press was the type it held. Although Robert Harling, the typographer, was to complain of the lack of enterprise of the English in designing new type, and to put down as merely 'fashionable' those seeking novelty from abroad, if that's what it took to be a pioneer, that's what Lund Humphries did. At the turn of the century it was investing heavily in new and varied type, irrespective of whether it was 'fashionable' to do so or not. The afore mentioned Yorkshire Industries Survey, described the company's composing room as having –

'...a splendid assortment of types, ornaments etc. from the best English, American and German type foundries.'

And when Edward's son Eric, a hard task-master, took the reins at Bradford, he made it a special mission to keep up to date when it came to type, as, for example, testing out each new face emerging from Monotype, and showing it off in what ever Lund Humphries was printing at the time. With Eric, it was said that 'something of the Bauhaus spirit rubbed off on the company composing room'. It was Eric who invited the avant garde typographer Jan Tschichold over to England, giving him an exhibition. Nicolas Barker was to praise Lund Humphries' skill in so ably grafting new type on to 'its solid English stock'.

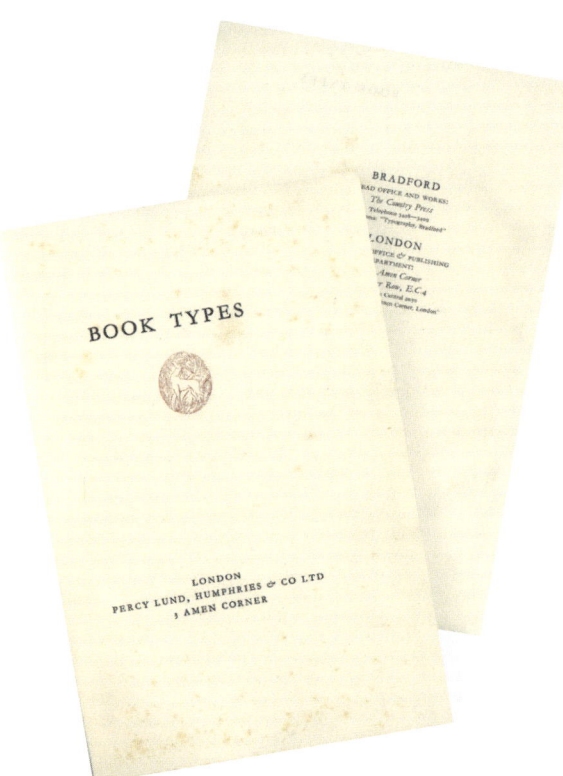

Above The Lund Humphries *Book Types*. 1920s text type comparison book.

The Bradford works

And then there was the arrival of Bruno Schindler as Publishing Manager during WWII. With him the company's stock of non-Roman fonts expanded exponentially, for as a sinologist and Middle East specialist he introduced Chinese and Arabic faces. The compositors, who were generally non-linguists, would, on occasion, have to send their work down to the School of African and Oriental Studies in London, for its students to check for accuracy. Eventually the Press was able to offer over eighty languages and to build up a reputation for foreign language printing.

When Herbert Spencer arrived, as typographical adviser, in the post-war years, he is said to have given the composing room an entire spring cleaning, ensuring the company maintained its reputation for being up-to-the-minute.

To handle its commissions and publishing Lund Humphries appears to have had a remarkably loyal and generally contented workforce, untroubled by union action, working through representative councils for its various departments. It is claimed that no-one was ever sacked. Lubelski, something of a partisan, but, nevertheless, someone who had actually interviewed past employees, wrote –

'The workforce actually enjoyed coming to work, actually enjoyed being part of the production team. The sense of satisfaction and fulfillment was a common and shared experience.'

The especially high standard of work of the press and the progressive stance of the company were part and parcel of Lund Humphries' reputation. Whenever the company was referred to in the press, 'quality' was an adjective almost always used, if not implied. Ruari McLean, the typographer, for example, wrote of his good fortune in getting a position in Bradford's composing room –

'the most forward-looking printing firm in Great Britain.'

Above Part of the Chinese composing department, c.1970s.

A pioneering printer

The Bradford works

Even in the late 1960s when all was not, perhaps, well with the company, a printing trade journalist wrote in *The British Printer*, still using an old form of the company's name –

'Why does Percy Lund, Humphries produce such superb quality printing.'

Although graphic design and printing historians tend to remember Lund Humphries for such shining stars as the *Penrose Annual*, *Typographica* and its monographs on contemporary artists (all to be described in later chapters), its reputation continually brought it commissions from blue-chip internationals as well as from more modest local clients for more standard, day-to-day printing requirements. From early local commissions as for the 1904 City of Bradford Great Exhibition and for the West Yorkshire Regiment, to post-WWII commissions for the grand auction houses of Sotheby's and Christie's, from local firms as Paton & Baldwin and Bradford & Bingley Building Society to the government agency – the Stationery Office, and to such internationals as I.C.I. and British Steel, the Works strove to maintain its standards, and its reputation, through to the end.

Above Design studio, c.1960s.

Opposite left Advertisment, *Penrose Annual*, 1961, showing the range of Lund Humphries foreign language typefaces, **Right** Advertisement from *Designers in Britain 5*, 1954, promoting the company's creative services.

Eric Beresford Humphries and Eric Craven (Peter) Gregory

Above *EMcKK*, catalogue for the 1954 memorial exhibition of the work by E.McKnight Kauffer at the V&A, organised by the Society of Industrial Artists. Printed by Lund Humphries. **Opposite** *Flight*, 1917, the woodcut by Edward McKnight Kauffer, was adapted in 1919 for *The Early Bird* poster to publicise the re-launch of the *Daily Herald*.

Lucy Myers, managing director of Lund Humphries Publishing Co. edited a small booklet on the history of the company as an art book publisher, which included a comment on the two –

'They were a dynamic duo. While Gregory cultivated relationships with the art world, it was Eric Humphries who brought technical printing knowledge to the partnership and an eye for modern typography.'

Although the division of responsibility may not have been quite so watertight as suggested, Eric Beresford Humphries (1894-1968) and Eric Craven Gregory (1888-1959) – to be here shortened to Eric to distinguish him from his father, and Gregory to distinguish him from his friend – were to steer Lund Humphries through some of its most brilliant years, from the 1920s to the 1960s.

In Edward Humphries will the two are each described as 'master printer', yet nothing is recorded of either having any formal training in either printing or design. The two are sometimes referred to as having been 'school friends' at Bradford Grammar School, which seems doubtful because of their age difference. Gregory had actually been born in Scotland, but to Yorkshire parents, who returned to their roots when he was still young. Both Eric and Gregory were loyal Yorkshiremen, Eric spending his life there, Gregory having a farmstead there even though his working base was to be in London.

The pair each appear to have joined Lund Humphries straight from school. There would have been no query about Eric joining his father's company, it would be a natural choice, but why the young Gregory is taken on is more problematic. The surmise his being Eric's school friend, even if this were true, is hardly a justified selection criterion. It has been suggested that Gregory had already demonstrated some of his admirable personality qualities, particularly his ease with people, whilst still at school, and this may well have been something that influenced his selection.

Both Eric and Gregory were to distinguish themselves, when enlisting during WWI – Gregory as a Captain in the 6th Battalion of the West Yorkshire Regiment, and Eric as a fighter pilot, who was awarded the Military Cross. On their return to the company, both were appointed to the Board of Directors, to become joint Managing Directors in 1930. Gregory, however, was appointed Chairman before Eric, who took on the role after Gregory's death in 1959.

They were as unalike in character as were Percy Lund and Edward Humphries. Lubelski contrasts them –

'Humphries was short, square but athletic, dynamic, red-faced, choleric, quick-tempered, married; Gregory, tall, elegant, thoughtful, even-tempered, a bachelor.'

Although in design and publishing history Gregory, in spite of being of a modest nature, actually hogs the limelight, those who knew the pair, and had worked at Lund Humphries, rated Eric as the real driving force, the company revolving around him; his Bradford operation

Above Eric Beresford Humphries 1894-1968.

underpinning Gregory's adventuring in the London art world.

Michael Clapham, a former employee in the 1930s, who had worked with Eric, encapsulated something of his style of operating –

'Mr.Eric is there already, red-faced and bursting with energy, he had generally run a mile or two before breakfast. He skims through the mail, throws out instructions, curses anyone who has not got the information he requires or worse is found not to have got a job done by the date promised, and eventually dismisses us all with our share of letters to answer.'

Eric was ever on the move, driving into work in his Lagonda sports car, snatching at every opportunity presenting itself, however demanding; and ever on the lookout for capital to implement his continuous flow of ideas.

Anthony Bell, deplored the fact that Eric was to be so frequently overlooked, offering a description of him –

'...having dynamism and technical flair, plus a rarely recognised but highly required eye for the modern idiom of typography...' and as 'bringing a new dynamic to the composing room'.

Without a standard apprenticeship Eric was to self-educate, when it came to printing and typography, keeping abreast of what was going on at home and abroad. He eagerly seized on any new typefaces emerging from such European foundries as Bauer, Stempel, and Ludwig & Mayer; as the artist/typographer Max Bill described it – 'attempting to bring some visual element to the wasteland of commercial printing'.

Above Eric Craven (Peter) Gregory 1888-1959.

THE GUEST

Tall, cool and gentle, you are here
To turn the water into wine.
Now, at the ebbing of the year,
Be you the sun we need to shine.

It is the birthday of your word;
And we are gathered. Will you come?
Let not your spirit be a sword,
O, luminous delightful lord.

HAROLD MONRO.

Eric Humphries and Peter Gregory

Eric's concern for the aesthetics as well as for the technicalities of printing is demonstrated when he wrote in the company's apprentice magazine *The Devil's Own** –

'Printing is not concerned with mass production of standardized articles: it is a living creative craft to which all branches make their individual contribution. We, of this Company, believe that, if we are interested in the creative side, our day's work passes more quickly and we go home with a greater sense of satisfaction than if we had been concerned with merely a mechanical aspect. I want you to understand the great importance we attach to the creative side.'

Eric was on a mission!

While Eric was rabble rousing his troops in the battle for high quality and aesthetic printing in Bradford, Gregory was active, but perhaps rather less obviously and less vigorously so, in London. As Eric was to educate himself on the typography and printing front, Gregory, a relatively uneducated youth when it came to 'art', was to become knowledgeable about, and, indeed, an activist on the behalf of, young contemporary British artists. It was Gregory who was to bring both Edward McKnight Kauffer (the American who was to dominate British graphic design in the inter-war years) and Herbert Spencer (to be a pioneer of 'modern' typography and primary lecturer in the subject at the Royal College of Art) into Lund Humphries as advisers; and it was Gregory's friendship with Henry Moore that was to start the company off on the path to becoming a leading art book publisher.

*Printing industry apprentices were known as 'Printers Devils'

Above *The Visible Word* written and designed by Herbert Spencer, printed and published by Lund Humphries, in association with the Royal College of Art, 1968.
Opposite *The Guest* by Harold Munro, Number four in a series of Christmas cards designed by Kauffer, printed and published by Lund Humphries & Co, in collaboration with the Poetry Bookshop, 1920s.

A pioneering printer

Through to his death, there was hardly an arts organization that Gregory was not linked to. He was in the founding group establishing The Institute of Contemporary Art; at various times was on the governing board of a number of art schools including St.Martin's, and Chelsea, and the Bath Academy; he served for various periods as director of the *Burlington Magazine*, as Chairman of the Ganymed Press, and on the Arts Council itself. Generally modest and low-key in what he did, Gregory allowed his name to be attached to the Gregory Fellowships in the Creative Arts at the University of Leeds in 1949, beneficiaries of which included Terry Frost, Alan Davie, Kenneth Armitage and Reg Butler.

Based at Lund Humphries' London office in Bedford Square for four days a week, Gregory created there what Anthony Bell described as 'a civilized ambience'. Philip Hendy, (Director of the Leeds Art Gallery and then the National Gallery), asserted that Gregory during his stewardship –

'...perhaps played a larger part in English art history of the past forty years than any other man who is not an artist.'

Although, as Lucy Myers characterized the period, Eric held the reins in Bradford, Gregory in London, each with their own enthusiasms, their own missions, Gregory was not an unfamiliar figure in the Works, and Eric was to be seen in London from time to time. At the Works there was a traffic light system to alert people to when they were needed elsewhere, and although Eric's red light would have been most frequently on, Gregory was allotted a green one, suggesting that his presence there was significant. He would visit regularly, no doubt his trips north having the additional attraction of his house there in the countryside. Eric's

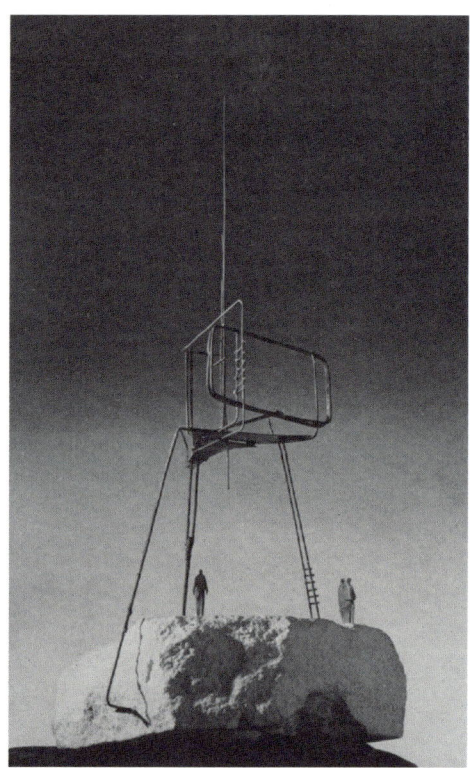

Above Original maquette for the *Monument to The Unknown Political Prisoner*, 1951-2, by Reg Butler, one of the beneficiaries of the Gregory Fellowships.

Above Catalogue for Ganymed Press and *below* Victoria and Albert Musuem catalogue, 1980.

Eric Humphries and Peter Gregory

visits to London would probably have included attendance at the Double Crown Club, an exclusive dining club for printers, publishers, and graphic designers, and through that he would have extended his printing network as, for example, his meeting with Oliver Simon of the Curwen Press, who was instrumental in Eric's using, at one time, the pioneering typographer Stanley Morison. And Eric was also involved in some of the exhibitions held in Bedford Square, particularly those concerned with typography, as that for Jan Tschichold, as well as having a hand in setting up a company design studio there. And then, together, the pair had ventured into post-war Germany to look at printing works, a technical matter, as a result of which Lund Humphries came to part own the Ganymed Press, to become notable for its fine reproductions of paintings – with Gregory a Director.

From such examples there can be seen to have been some blurring of the boundary between London and Bradford, for Eric became a crusader for making printing an art form; and, of course, Gregory would have had to have had a sufficient knowledge of the running of the Works when negotiating commissions. Both Eric and Gregory were 'modernists', determined that whatever Lund Humphries did it should be up-to-date if not ahead of the field. In spite of their contrasting personalities they appear to have worked amicably in harness and to have established what, in hindsight, was to be the company's 'golden age'.

The London base

Above 3 Amen Corner. Lund Humphries' name is visible above the doorway.
Opposite Invitation to an exhibition of 55 years of printing held at Bedford Square 1939.

Percy Lund might be said to have been more motivated by his many passions than by personal financial gain. Nevertheless when it came to proselytizing, whether for his interests or his business, he seems to have been no slouch when it came to marketing. He appreciated that having a base in London would be advantageous to his company not only by possibly attracting larger and more sophisticated commissions, but by the fact that a London address would balance the more homely image given by 'The Country Press' that was to be an addition to the firm's name through much of its existence.

As early as 1886 Percy took possession of 3 Amen Corner, in a terrace of 17th century buildings designed to give accommodation to the clergy of St.Paul's nearby. Little is recorded of the firm's occupancy of the building, but it must have served its purpose of gaining more printing commissions reasonably well enough, for it was not until 1932 that Lund Humphries felt it had outgrown the place and made its momentous move to 12 Bedford Square.

Bedford Square not only gave the company more space but changed its image, for the Square was, and is, one of the most impressive in London. The Georgian houses, built in the late 1770s, have an imposing uniformity, the middle house on each side particularly impressive with a pediment. The actual visual impact of the Square would have added to Lund Humphries' brand image, but, additionally,

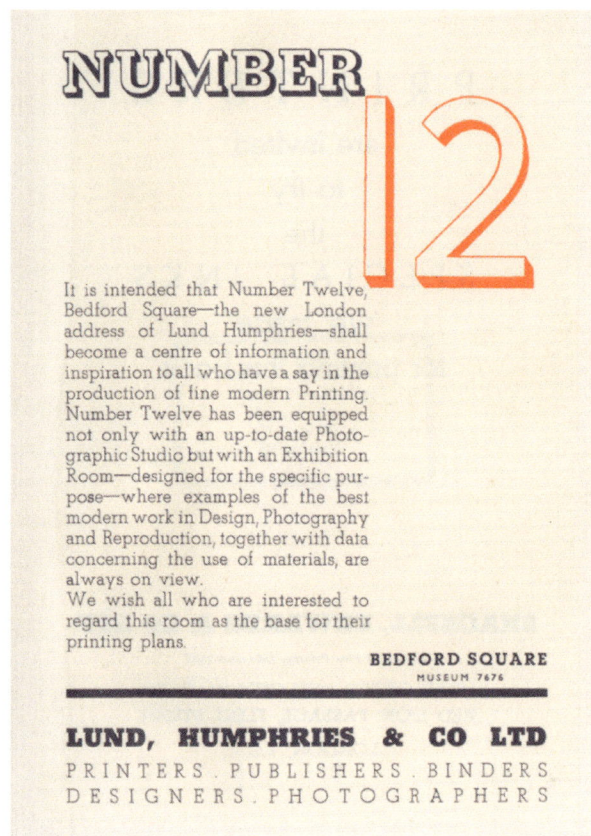

Above Advertisement announcing Lund Humphries move to Bedford Square.

Above 12 Bedford Square.

Below Change of address card designed by Kauffer, featuring a photogram influenced by Man Ray.

moving there associated the company with cultured intelligentsia and up-market publishing. To-day the Square is littered with blue plaques including those of the publishers Frederick Warne & Co. (publishers of Beatrix Potter), and Jonathan Cape; whilst across from no.12 was the Architectural Association, the old-established architectural school which had moved there in 1917. Other distinguished inhabitants of the Square, at one time or another, were Edward Lutyens, Herbert Asquith and Ottoline Morrell, the Bloomsbury hostess.

No.12 is a substantial building of four floors and a basement, the first with decorative balconies. The ground floor, initially conceived of as a sales space, was soon designated as one to be used for exhibitions. The overall design for this was carried out by Hall, Easton & Robertson, the last being Principal of the Architectural Association; with Marion Dorn, McKnight Kauffer's partner, designing the curtains and flooring. The other floor, that was to add to Lund Humphries' reputation, was the basement, which included a studio and dark room, with photographic equipment. The basement was freely available to graphic designers who wished to use it. McKnight Kauffer, appointed Design Director by Gregory, did much of his work there until returning to America at the onset of war; indeed he did work for companies other than Lund Humphries, to be printed by other presses, such was Gregory's generosity and close friendship.

For a time the basement also gave shelter to the American photographer Man Ray. It was Man Ray's photographic experiments that had actually influenced Kauffer's design of the company's change of address card. As artists and designers began to frequent the ground floor and the basement, elsewhere in the building Lund Humphries decided to install its own studio. The work of the company's own artists went largely unacknowledged by name, albeit some had remarkable

Above Cresset Press catalogue, 1927-1934. Designed by Maurice Bennett. Text pages printed matt black, with printed celluloid overlays and cover. Produced to coincide with the Cresset Press exhibition, 1934, at Lund Humphries' Bedford Square Gallery.

The London Base

Above Swan Court, Chelsea.
Below Swan Court Blue Plaque.

talent, as Maurice Bennett, who had been inveigled in from the Crawford advertising agency. Design began to dictate the tune.

Although Amen Corner and Bedford Square were to be the 'official' London bases for Lund Humphries, an 'unofficial' one was to be Swan Court in Swan Walk, Chelsea. Swan Court was a smart, expensive block of flats, built in 1931. On the 8th floor were studio flats, and as soon as letting opened Kauffer and Marion Dorn moved into a double studio, nos.139 and 141, which had a balcony running round it. Who rented first is not clear, but Gregory became their neighbour across the hall. The Kauffer and Dorn studio was described as immaculate – white linoleum, built-in plain wood furniture, Dorn curtains and rugs, friend's paintings and sculpture – everything in its place. In contrast Gregory's was 'an utter confusion', overflowing with scattered books and pictures. Presumably when he moved into the Kauffer's flat when they had returned to America, chaos also reigned there, for it was reputed to have been something of a challenge to the Lund Humphries' staff who volunteered to clear it on Gregory's death. One can only wonder how the two different styles of operating of Kauffer and Gregory, worked together so apparently amicably when it came to commissions.

In addition to the Kauffers and Gregory, Swan Court had other occupants with connections to the company – John Hayward, (an American photographer and friend of T.S.Eliot), Francis Brugiere (with whom Kauffer worked on commissions and for whom Lund Humphries mounted an exhibition), and Hans Schleger, another Kauffer friend who also was given an exhibition in Bedford Square. A blue plaque now records the Kauffer's stay there. Swan Court could be said to have been a Lund Humphries 'cell', for the occupants, oftimes spending their leisure together, would surely have included hatching plans for no.12.

Penrose Annual

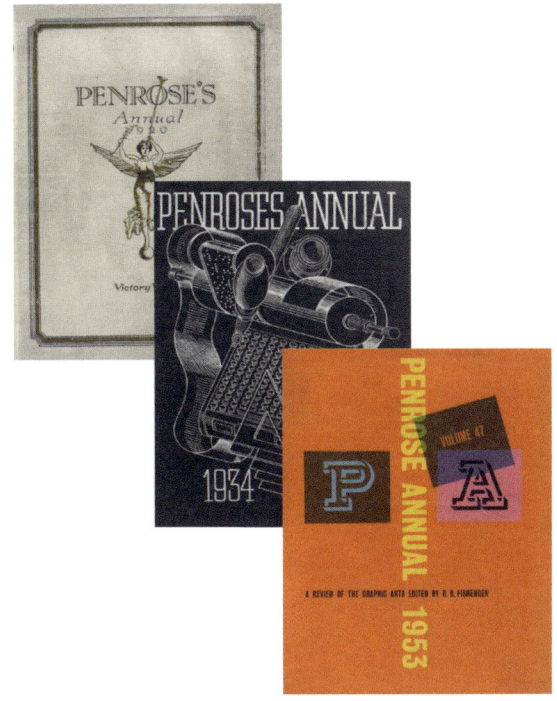

Above *Penrose Annual*, 1920, *Victory Volume*, 1934, and 1953 covers and wrappers.
Opposite Title page for what was to become the *Penrose Annual*, 1900.

When Percy Lund accepted what would seem to have been a fairly run-of-the-mill job, printing what was little more than a company's sales catalogue, he would have had no idea that this 'catalogue' would morph into a major international annual on printing and the graphic arts, with which his firm's name would be forever associated – the *Penrose Annual*.

In the 1880s a young William Gamble decided to chance his luck by coming to London. He had worked on the *Scarborough Daily Post* as a printer turned sub-editor, and had conceived of the possibility of setting up a technical company for syndicating articles, including images, to provincial newspapers. Gamble was a self-motivated enthusiast, much as Percy Lund himself, and after several false starts, he decided to go it alone.

The process involved was highly technical and Gamble was soon attending courses on optics, chemistry and engineering and setting up a laboratory at home to experiment in possible methods of print transmission. Facing problems in getting supplies Gamble, in 1892, met a pharmaceutical chemist, A.W.Penrose, and, in no time, in 1893, the pair had established a company in Baker Street, with Gamble as both Director and Chairman, to supply materials and equipment to the printing industry.

It was this company that began to issue a monthly trade circular *Process Work*, to provide information on 'the latest novelties and development in process work'. This publication grew into a regular trade journal *Process Work and the Printer*. By 1895 the entrepreneurial Gamble had converted this into *The Process Work Yearbook* of which about a third was text and some two-thirds a Penrose catalogue. In the following year it carried the sub-title *The Penrose Annual*. Although initially Gamble had tried out another printer for this, he soon settled for Lund Humphries and the *Penrose's Pictorial Annual – the Process Year Book – a review of the graphic arts*, soon to be shortened to the *Penrose Annual*, was to be printed thereafter in Bradford; Lund Humphries was not only to be its printer but its proprietor when it bought the annual in 1909.

Gamble remained the Annual's editor until 1933, being succeeded by Richard Fishenden, who wrote of the happy collaboration between editor and proprietor and of Gamble's unique combination of talents –

'...he possessed in rare combination a well-balanced technical mind, sound business acuity, and a remarkable skill in the use of the written word.'

The Annual soon settled down into what was to become a familiar format – an initial review by the editor of what had gone on in the printing world that year (often extremely lengthy), a series of articles on technical and graphic concerns, examples of good practice and advertising. The Annual appears quickly to have been appreciated as a profitable place to advertise by many players in the printing world and its suppliers – from manufacturers of inks, paper and glues to machinery, along with the occasional advertisement from a technical college and even from artists themselves – all of which must have made a major contribution to keeping the Annual financially afloat.

Above Menu cover, 1937, for Simpsons of Piccadilly. Designed by Ashley Havinden for W S Crawford Advertising. Printed as an insert in Penrose 39 by Lund Humphries.

Penrose Annual

The early Annuals were largely technical in content, but, by the 1930s nearly half the articles were on graphic design rather than printing, and this ratio was to continue, linking Lund Humphries to both activities. The balance seems to have been achieved under Fishenden's editorship. He had been 'discovered' by Gamble when visiting the newly opened Manchester Municipal School of Technology, where Fishenden was teaching in the Photographic and Printing Crafts Department. Gamble soon got Fishenden contributing articles to the Annual of which he became the editor in 1934, continuing as such through to his death in 1956. Fishenden brought considerable printing know-how to the editorship and, additionally, had a strong interest in graphic design.

There was an early example of naming the designer for a particular Annual when it came to typography, when Eric brought in Stanley Morison to work on the 1923 issue introducing Monotype's 'Garamond' to the printing world. An unsigned review of this was laudatory –

> *'The twenty-fifth volume of the Penrose Annual comes with surprise. It has been stirred, as if by the kiss of fine typography to a consciousness of the position it holds; it has awakened into eminence, beauty and character.'*

From 1923 through to the late 1930s the Annual was to use the latest Monotype faces, and Fishenden was to involve, in succession, Robert Harling, Frederick A.Horn, Jan Tschichold, Francis Meynell and Richard de la Mare (of Faber & Faber) as Annual designers, insisting that the designer should be named and therefore recognized for their talent.

Such was the amicable nature of Lund Humphries proprietorial relationship with the Annual's editors that only four held that position until the Annual was sold – Gamble from 1895 to 1933; Fishenden

Above Menu design, 1937, by L. Moholy Nagy. For the farewell dinner for Walter Gropius. Printed by Lund Humphries and included as an insert in Penrose 40.

A pioneering printer

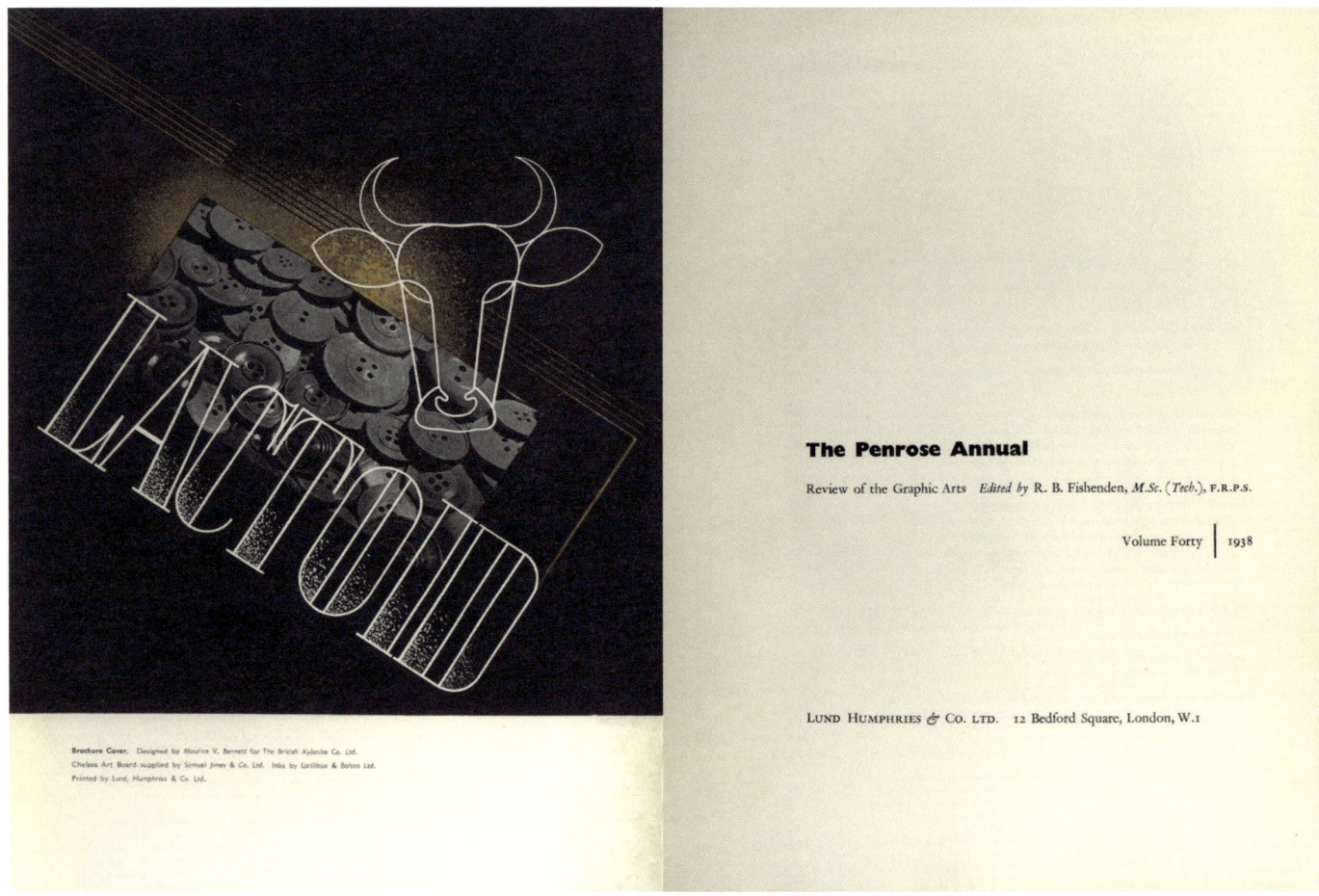

Above Penrose Annual 40, 1938. Frontispiece *Lactoid*, British Xylonite Co. Ltd., brochure cover designed by Maurice Bennett and printed by Lund Humphries.
Right Title page design and typography of the annual by Jan Tschichold.

Above and right Type specimen pages of current display typefaces, including *Offenbach*, Rudolf Koch's last type design, selected by Robert Harling, as an insert specially printed by Lund Humphries, for Penrose Annual 40, 1938.

from 1934 to 1956; Alan Delafons (a friend of Fishenden) from 1958 to 1962; and Herbert Spencer from 1967 to 1973. All were progressive in their stance – from Gamble's impatience with the slowness of the industry to make use of new ideas and new processes, through Fishenden wanting the industry to have a greater interest in aesthetics, to Spencer, perhaps the most progressive of all when it came to design, his editorship overlapping with his teaching at the Royal College of Art. Contributors, over the years, read as a roll call of the most exciting printers, typographers and designers of the time – including, along with those mentioned, Thomas Griffitts, James Shand, Milner Gray, Ashley Havinden, Moholy Nagy, and Beatrice Warde.

Apart from Eric's intervention with Garamond, and an early announcement in the 1905 issue that –

'The type throughout the text has been composed by Messrs. Percy Lund, Humphries & Co. Ltd on the Lanston Monotype.'

Lund Humphries was discrete in its ownership. Nevertheless its name would appear in each volume, on the title page and backing it, as proprietor and printer; the 1949 edition stated clearly 'design, printing and binding by Lund Humphries'.

Nevertheless, behind its modesty the company could be described as feverishly involved, for although the contents and editing were in other hands, the physical compiling of articles and illustrations, the binding in of inserts, the choice of paper, inks and binding, all occupied the Works during the year, and a small team was assigned solely to handle the production and to progress it along with other Lund Humphries work. As Lubelski wrote –

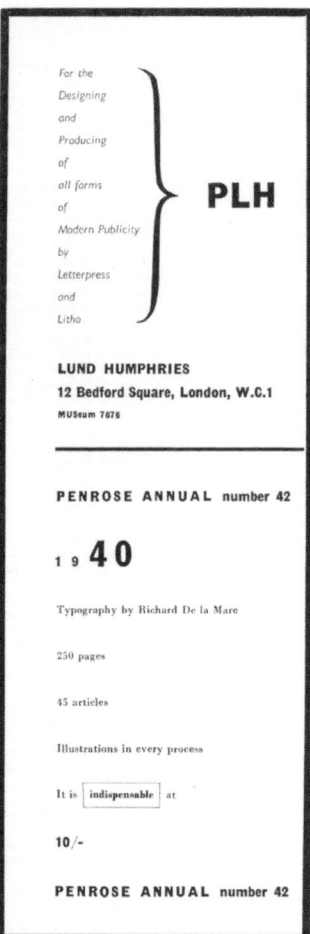

Above Advertisement for Lund Humphries in *Modern Publicity*, 1939-1940.

'…the Annual was going to be read, handled, examined, perused, evaluated, criticized, praised or otherwise by the entire graphic arts fraternity; thus the imperative to 'get it perfect'.

The Annual had barely any publishing competitors during the time of its long ownership by Lund Humphries, although, in the 1930s a Charles Knights had made a short-lived attempt with the *Print Users' Yearbook*. And although *Modern Publicity*, published by Studio Books, carried more international illustrations, it had an altogether narrower focus on graphic design alone.

The Annual gave Lund Humphries image a gloss, shinier than most other printers, associating it with progressiveness and with the graphic arts. Its title morphing, over the years, from *The Process Work Yearbook* to *The Penrose Graphic Arts International Annual* encapsulates what occurred under Lund Humphries guardianship. It was published until 1974 when it was sold to Northwood Publications, part of the Thompson Corporation; it ceased publication in 1982.

Above The 1969 *Penrose Annual* drying out under pressure at the Bradford Works.

 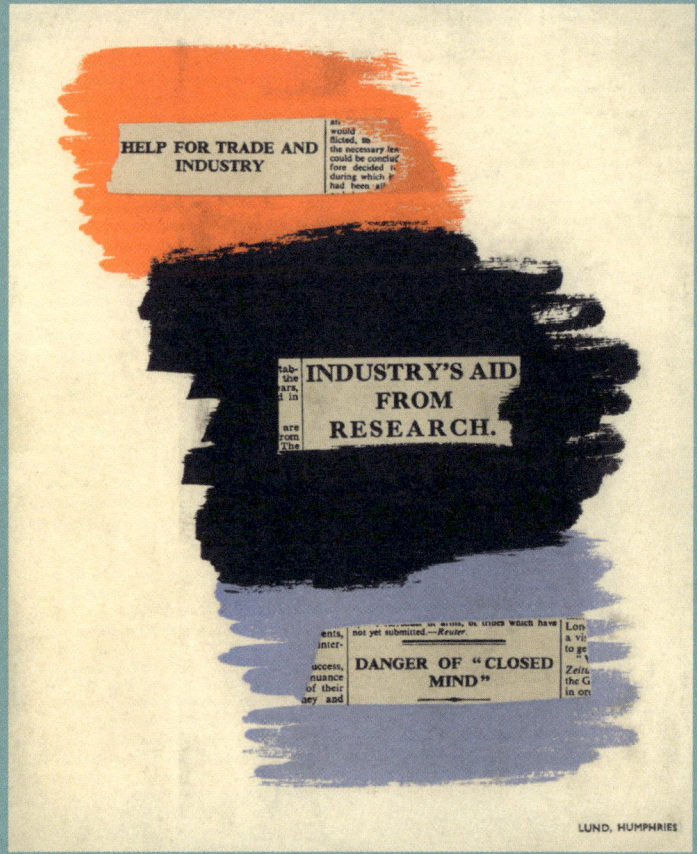

The Bedford Square exhibitions

In 1934, *Commercial Art*, then one of the leading journals on graphic design, included an article headed 'A Printer's Gallery of Ideas'. It considered it newsworthy that –

'a printer should hold exhibitions of the work of the best commercial artists in the country at frequent intervals is almost without precedent.'

The article went on to suggest that such events would not only be of interest to the public but could stimulate Lund Humphries' own 'capable and imaginative artists'. It concluded that –

'only such a firm who pays such attention to co-operation and experimentation as does Percy Lund, Humphries can worthily be called creative.'

Lund Humphries began mounting it's exhibitions soon after it's relocation to Bedford Square, and was to continue with them fairly regularly up to the onset of the Second World War, and occasionally after, into the 1960s.

The exhibitions can roughly be allocated to two groupings – commercial art/photography and typography – the former where the

Above The Bedford Square gallery. Curtains and carpet designed by Marion Dorn.
Opposite *EMcKK*, catalogue for his exhibition at Bedford Square, 1935. The introduction was reprinted from an article by Roger Fry.

hand of McKnight Kauffer is writ large; the latter more the province of Eric and of Herbert Spencer. Of course Gregory would have had to rubber stamp them during his reign at Bedford Square.

A glance at the early 'commercial art' exhibitions in the 1930s shows a varied, but rather odd assortment of personalities – the photographers-cum-artists Man Ray and Francis Bruguière, the graphic designers Hans Schleger, Lewitt-Him, and three transient Australians – Dahl and Geoffrey Collins (a couple) and Alastair Morison. The most puzzling of the commercial exhibitions mounted was that of 1934, just titled 'Exhibition of Commercial Design'. This included Edward Bawden, Rex Whistler, and Francis Marshall (the fashion illustrator), along with the rarity of two women commercial artists, R. Fran Sutton and Stella Steyn – a grouping that certainly had never been shown together before, nor did it ever appear together afterwards – an eccentric one-off.

The link between such a rag-bag was McKnight Kauffer, for although it is not recorded in every instance how he had met these artists, he was renowned for his generosity in sponsoring young designers new to the British public. Two of the artists receiving exhibitions were Man Ray, a fellow American, whose short experimental films Kauffer had managed to get shown in London, and who obtained portraiture commissions for him for the likes of T.S.Eliot and Aldous Huxley; and Hans Schleger, who Kauffer introduced to several of his own clients including Shell and London Transport.

It has been suggested that Kauffer first met Man Ray in Paris, when Kauffer was travelling at the time. Another American photographer, Francis Bruguière, who was to share an exhibition with Kauffer, was a neighbour at Swan Court although they had known each other earlier. Kauffer, himself, was interested in photography and with

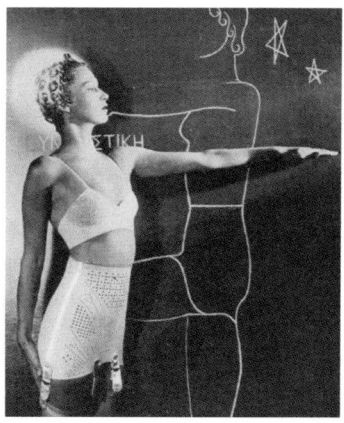

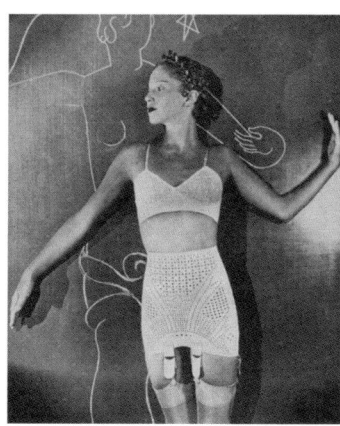

Above Photography for Charnaux Corset advertisements by Bruguière with background drawings by Kauffer, reproduced for their Bedford Square exhibition in 1933.

The Bedford Square exhibitions

the experimenting of both Ray and Bruguière – the latter with multi-exposures as early as the 1910s, the former with his Rayographs in the 1920s and 30s. Kauffer was to work on a number of advertising commissions with Bruguière for Charnaux and Spey Royal as well as for a mural for the Modernist Embassy Court flats in Brighton.

It was, perhaps, Kauffer's solo exhibition at No.12 that attracted most press coverage. He had already shown with Bruguière in Lund Humphries first Bedford Square exhibition in 1933, but in 1935 was given a solo show. The *Scotsman* named him 'The Picasso of Design' and a full appreciation of his work was provided by Anthony Blunt –

> *'Mr. McKnight Kauffer is an artist who makes me resent the division of the arts into major and minor…as I looked around the exhibition of his work at Messrs. Lund Humphries galleries in Bedford Square I was led to think "If he is minor, who then is major at any rate among his English contemporaries."'*

That McKnight Kauffer was allowed to run free, as it were, at Bedford Square, was not only due to his outstanding design skills and general usefulness to Lund Humphries in an advisory capacity, but to his close friendship to Gregory, who was to diary his 'great loss' when the Kauffers returned to America at the beginning of the war.

Eventually Lund Humphries got round to the fact that it could use the exhibition space to exhibit its own creativity, when, before the onset of Second World War, it mounted an exhibition to celebrate fifty-five years of the company's existence.

It was not only the exhibitions themselves that raised Lund Humphries' profile, but the graphics accompanying them – the invitation cards and catalogues (some of which Kauffer was to design).

Above and over the page The dotted line leads to the artists' invitation for the Lewitt Him exhibition, 1937.

A pioneering printer

LUND HUMPHRIES invite you to an Exhibition of Commercial Art and of Illustrations for Books by **LEWITT** and **HIM** to be held at 12, Bedford Square, London, W.C.1, from November 24 to December 15

● 12, Bedford Square, W.C.1

Above Announcement of an exhibition of Commercial Art, including work by Edward Bawden and Rex Whistler, 1937.

The Bedford Square exhibitions

The card for the Lewitt Him (Jan Le Witt and George Him) exhibition is one most frequently cited for its humour for it portrayed the pair as paint brushes of different thicknesses representing their contrasting builds, but with a shared handle/torso. Kauffer wrote of them –

'They are comic, they are amusing, they are thoughtful, they are serious, and they are good advertising.'

Schleger designed his own catalogue, but others were done by Frederick Horn (who by-the-by contributed articles on typography for the Penrose Annual), and by Lund Humphries' own designer, Maurice Bennett, who also designed for other London exhibitions as for one on Picasso held at Zwemmer's art gallery in 1936. Anthony Bell reflecting back on this inter-war period felt that Bennett had been badly overlooked –

'Many of the outstanding successes have been designed by Maurice Bennett of our own studio; but such is the nature of typography, and rightly so, in the opinion of many well-qualified to judge, among the most brilliant designers in England must often remain anonymous, cloaked under the imprint Lund Humphries... a man handling modern types and modern layout forms, takes every corner with the sure touch of Nuvolari*, he has made good taste a very positive value.'

More Eric's province, were two exhibitions of typography mounted prior to the onset of war – one celebrating the typographer Rudolf Koch and the type foundry Klingspor with which he had his distinguished

---

*Nuvolari was an Italian racing driver

A pioneering printer

MAN RAY

will be at 12 Bedford Square W.C.1 from
December 5th to December 15th 1935

Intelligent photography by a brilliant artist
commissions are invited for portraits,
and all other subjects.

museum 7676
LUND HUMPHRIES

Above and Opposite Invitations designed by Maurice Bennett for the 1935 Man Ray and 1936 Picasso exhibitions.

PICASSO

The honour of your company is requested at a Private View of important paintings of all periods and other works by Pablo Picasso on Wednesday, 20th May, 1936, at the Zwemmer Gallery, 26 Litchfield Street, W.C.2. Tel.: Temple Bar 1793. The Exhibition finishes 20th June.

LUND HUMPHRIES

career; the other on a very much alive typographer, Jan Tschichold.

Karl Klingspor was the driving force that had taken a provincial foundry in Offenbach and built it into one with an international reputation. He had pioneered the commission of artists to design type and although using a number of others, Koch was the one longest in his employ. He was to design some thirty new type faces and perhaps was distinguished by his name attached to the title of the Lund Humphries exhibition because of his recent death in 1934. Eric was familiar with the Klingspor type range, particularly with Koch's Neuland, which was well-suited to commercial work and had begun to be used in England from the 1920s. It is possible that Eric may have heard Koch speak at a Double Crown Club dinner in 1930, when he had been made an honorary member. The exhibition was curated by Robert Harling, still only in his twenties, and who had worked at Lund Humphries on his way to becoming typographic adviser to the *Sunday Times*, proprietor of the journal *Alphabet & Image* and, eventually editor of *House & Garden*.

It is generally recorded that Lund Humphries invited Jan Tschichold to London, (one assumes this was by Eric). Tschichold was, perhaps, one of the best known 'modernist' typographers in Europe at the time, and the company not only gave him his first exhibition in Britain, in 1935, but commissioned him to redesign its stationery, and, in 1938, to design the *Penrose Annual* of that year. After the war he was to return to London to shake up the typography at Penguin Books. Influenced by Bauhaus teaching he became best known for his asymmetrical designs which he wrote on in *Die Neue Typographie*. It was when the young Ruari Maclean was working as an assistant manager in the Lund Humphries composing room in Bradford, that he came across some of the remains of what had been on show in

Above A Klingspor device, 1950s.
Below Rudolf Koch Kabel Book, upper and lowercase, Klingspor type foundry, 1926.

The Bedford Square exhibitions

Above *Typography in Britain today* exhibition, 1963.
Below Catalogue for the exhibition.
Both designed by Herbert Spencer.

the London exhibition and, consequently, became obsessed with Tschichold's work, eventually writing a book on him.

It was not until Herbert Spencer joined Lund Humphries in an advisory role that further typographical exhibitions were mounted at Bedford Square. In 1952, aided by Anthony Bell (to become Lund Humphries' Chairman), *Purpose & Pleasure* was organised, drawing on typographical designers from across the world, including Max Bill and Jan Tschichold from Switzerland and Paul Rand from the States. Rick Poynor, the typographical design historian, saw the exhibition as –

'the most concentrated statement in Britain, up to that time, for the contemporary style.'

Some ten years on, in 1963, Spencer mounted an even more ambitious typographical exhibition – *Typography in Britain today*, for which some thirty seven designers were invited to choose a selection of their work and present it, how they would, on display panels (Spencer had at least three for his own work). This enabled a new generation of typographers and graphic designers to be on show to the public, and included Alan Fletcher, Derek Birdsall, Peter Wildbur and George Daulby.

The exhibitions at Bedford Square, attracting the great and the good, brought considerable kudos to Lund Humphries, adding to its image as a design-conscious, progressive printer. But the cost of mounting the exhibitions was by no means offset by the mere dribble of commissions resulting from them. Kauffer gained a few for himself and Anthony Bell a few for Lund Humphries; Lewitt-Him got their first commissions in England. As with other Lund Humphries secondary activities the considerable prestige gained was rarely accompanied by the costs being covered, let alone profit being made.

A pioneering printer

Exhibition invitations and catalogues, printed by Lund Humphries for other galleries

Right Mayor Gallery *Art Now* Catalogue, 1933, with an introduction by Herbert Read. Design by Kauffer.

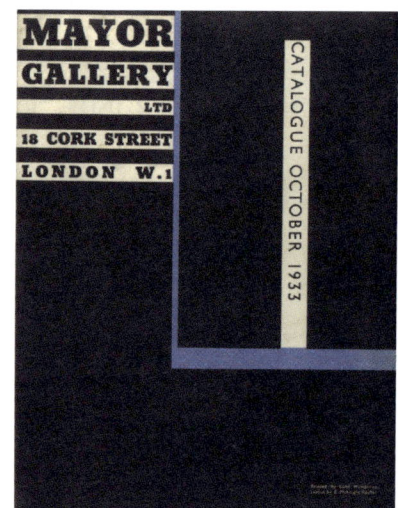
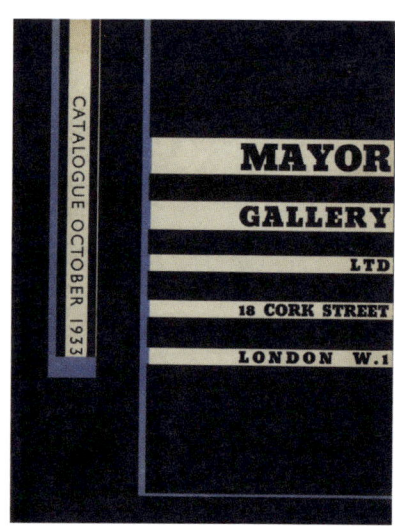

Below Edvard Munch at the London Gallery, Munch's first exhibition in London. Invitation design by Ashley Havinden.

The Bedford Square exhibitions

Left Exhibition Pictures in Advertising by Shell-Mex and B.P. Ltd, 1934, catalogue design by Kauffer.

Right Shell-Mex & B.P. Ltd. exhibition of Pictures in Advertising, 1938. Catalogue design by Kauffer.

Herbert Spencer and Typographica

Rick Poynor, the biographer of the journal *Typographica*, tells of the chance happening that brought it, one of the most stimulating journals on typography and the graphic arts produced in Britain in the early post-war years, into existence –

'Typographica came into being because an individual – Spencer, wanted it to exist and was lucky enough to encounter a publisher prepared to underwrite his youthful project, while leaving it entirely in his hands.'

The 'youth' was Herbert Spencer; the publisher Peter Gregory. Spencer, a Londoner by birth and upbringing, brought with him no formal qualifications of accreditation when he approached Gregory with his idea for a journal. He had been interested in printing since childhood, had bought himself a hand press, and had picked up what knowledge and skills he could by dipping into a variety of courses offered by the Regent Street School, Bolt Court and Toynbee Hall.

'I became passionately interested in printing at the age of 12. I don't remember what started it off or why printing has this extraordinary fascination for me.'

Above Advertisement in *Penrose Annual*, 1953.
Opposite *Typographica 2*, 1950. Edited by Herbet Spencer, cover lettering by Imre Reiner.

A pioneering printer

For a short time between leaving school and joining up for war service Spencer worked for the advertising agency Cecil B Notley. And after his service as a RAF cartographer in its Photo Interpretation Unit, he joined the London Typographical Designers (LTD), putting his hand to whatever commissions came along, whether catalogues or stationery or trade marks (designing one for Marconi). In 1948, deciding to take a risk, Spencer went free-lance, which was virtually unknown for typographers at that time.

It was as a free-lance Spencer was invited by the artist Alfred Rozelaar-Green to devise a typography course to be put on at his Anglo-French Art Centre cum Art School in St.John's Wood. Rozelaar-Green, after some time at the Central School of Arts and Crafts, had completed his training in Paris ateliers, and it was this experience that inspired him to set up his centre 'to revolutionise art education' in Britain. One can only describe what went on there as 'fluid' – students could come and go as they would and study what they wanted for as long as they wanted; visiting 'tutors' could take what role interested them – running courses, giving a one-off lecture, criticizing work, presenting awards, and so on. Such personalities as Leger and Kokoschka came over from the Continent, whilst British visitors and students included Jacob Epstein, Henry Moore, Francis Bacon, Graham Sutherland and Victor Pasmore.

It was in such a milieu that the young Spencer laid on his typography course, introducing it with a crusading prospectus –

'to encourage, through experiment and wide research, the production and appreciation of work that is in harmony with the conditions of our time. It will avoid the imitation or creation of any style and will seek to prove that a dance-

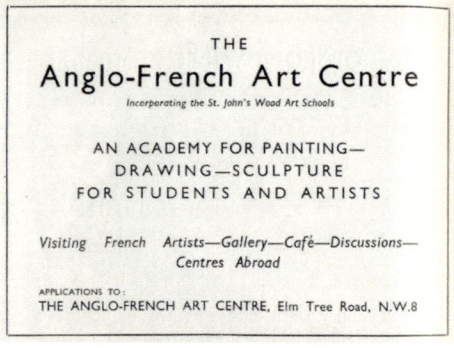

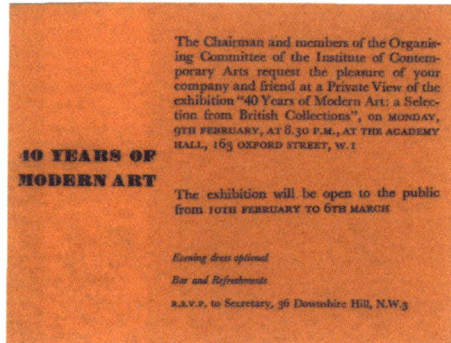

Above Advertisement for the Anglo-French Art Centre in which Spencer taught his typography course.
Below Private view invitation card for *40 Years of Modern Art* exhibition, 1948. Commissioned by Eric Gregory from Herbert Spencer.

Herbert Spencer and Typographica

ticket or trade-card can be a true expression of the art of typography no less than a limited edition'.

It was this prospectus that came to the attention of Gregory, who promptly arranged to meet young Spencer and to offer him a commission to produce some of the graphics for the opening exhibition of the Institute of Contemporary Arts, which Gregory had helped establish and was to subsidise.

Encouraged by such a positive interest in his work, Spencer showed Gregory a dummy of a journal he wanted to publish, asking if Lund Humphries would distribute it. Poynor tells of Gregory's immediate response –

'My boy, you're going to lose a lot of money. I'll publish it for you'.

On such an impulse Lund Humphries published, printed and distributed *Typographica* for nearly twenty years, from 1949 to 1967.

The journal came out in two blocks of issues each containing sixteen numbers, with print runs of usually less than three thousand. It had been planned that each would come out every few months, but this Spencer found difficult to sustain whilst building up a career in teaching and free-lance work, particularly as he was both editor and contributor, preparing every issue minutely marked up ready for Bradford to print. He was to admit that at the beginning he was 'flying by the seat of his pants', making what use he could of any ideas coming to him or those suggested by others. Ken Garland, the graphic designer, was to describe Spencer as 'a magpie' in his search for arresting material.

Above *Typographica* prospectus, c.1948. Spencer's design was later used as the cover for *Typographica* 3 and printed in black and yellow.

A pioneering printer

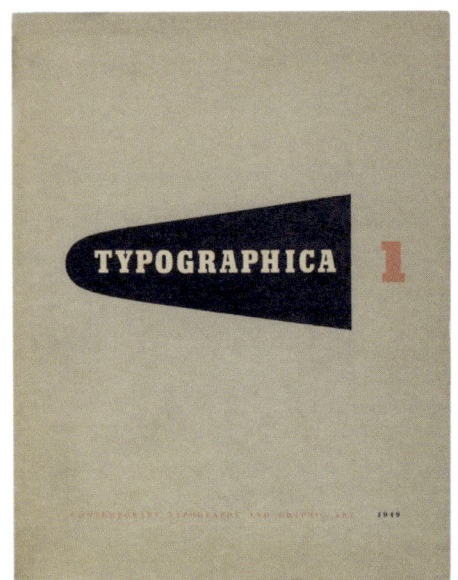

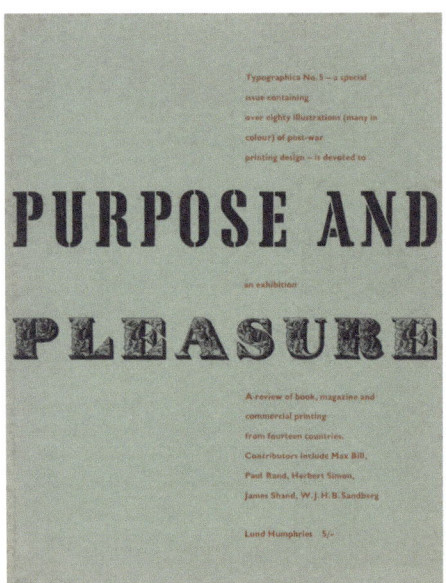

Above *Typographica* 1, 1949. Herbert Spencer in his preface describes the purpose of *Typographica* as a serious analysis of contemporary typography - aesthetic, technical and experimental.

Above *Typographica* 5, devoted to *Purpose and Pleasure*, the exhibition of post war book, magazine and commercial printing design from fourteen countries. held at Bedford square, 1952.

Above *Typographica* 14, late 1957. Publications of *Typographica* became less regular towards the end of its run due to external pressures. There were to be two more issues.

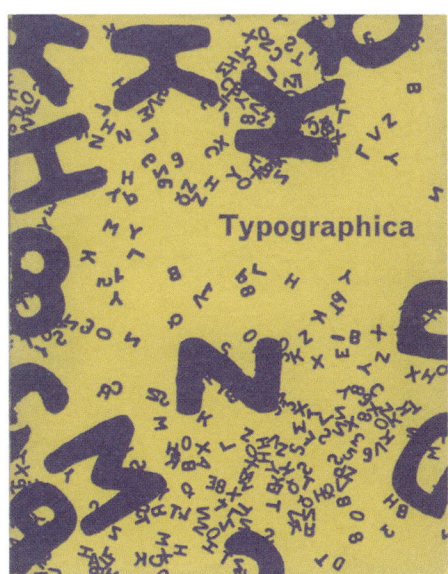

Above *Typographica*, new series, no.1, June 1960. Spencer continued his plan to include a wide coverage of experimental and international typography. The cover design is from a photogram of pasta letters by Anne Hickmott.

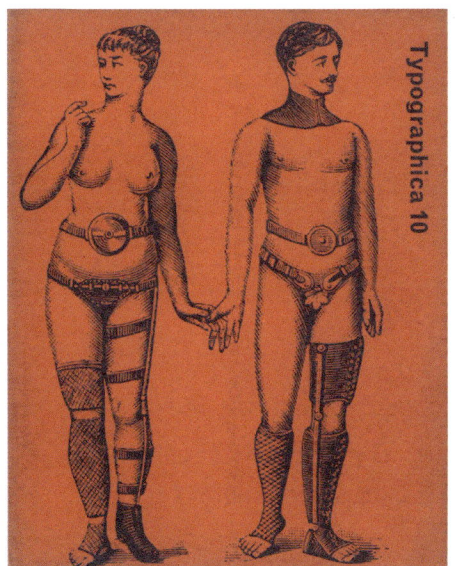

Above *Typographica*, new series, no.5, December 1964. Includes an article on 'Sex and Typography' by Robert Brownjohn who describes the film titles for James Bond films; *From Russia with Love* and *Goldfinger*.

Above *Typographica*, new series, no.16, December 1967, the final issue. Originally the magazine was printed by letterpress and later issues printed with litho sections. The cover is from a letter by Kurt Schwitters.

A pioneering printer

The thirty-two issues covered every aspect of printing and the graphic arts from common or garden ephemera to international typographic pioneering, printed in red, white and black, the arresting colours of the Constructivists. Whilst British publications on typography and printing such as *Alphabet & Image* and *Signature* tended to be a little more parochial, Spencer was a committed internationalist, albeit leaning more to Europe than to America.

Typographica seems to have become something of an ego-trip for Spencer and, without a firm hand from Lund Humphries, it would often contain wildly eccentric matters, along with an increasing number of photographs, many taken by Spencer, himself, when photography became something of an passion with him.

As *Penrose Annual* was to provide Lund Humphries with a raised profile within the printing industry and only later on with graphic designers and publishers, *Typographica* was, from the start, to attract the attention of art schools and designers. It came to be distributed to over twenty five countries and only ceased in 1967 when Spencer felt he had said all he wanted to say about the 'marriage' of word and image and Lund Humphries confronted its role as financial subsidiser of a project that brought fame but little profit.

Nevertheless Spencer proved of value to the company in a broader way for, in 1950, he was appointed its typographical consultant, and from 1964 until 1973, was to edit *Penrose Annual*; in 1969 he was made a director. As a consultant he visited the Bradford works monthly, and although a very modest, gentle, rather diffident character, soon did a spring clean of the company's type, and, only a year into his advisory role, in 1951, compiled a House Rules handbook. The Bradford work force of hardened printers appears to have responded positively to the odd situation of being directed by a young designer from London.

Above *Typographica*, new series, no.7, May 1963, printed to coincide with the *Typography in Britain Today* exhibition.
Below Invitation, 1965, to an exhibition featuring 'a cross section of the work reproduced in *Typraphica*, since 1949'. Held at Monotype House, Fetter Lane, London.

Herbert Spencer and Typographica

Spencer was to work on numerous books for Lund Humphries and saw that it extended its publishing to include typographic and design titles as well as those on contemporary artists.

As Kauffer was to influence what was going on, at least at the London end of Lund Humphries, in the inter-war years, Spencer was to be the major aesthetic influence in the post-war period, bringing sophistication and a further internationalism to Lund Humphries pioneering image.

Above *House Rules* 1951, compiled by Herbert Spencer.

'*Mister Moore, Mister Nicholson and Mister Nash to see you*' amused aside in a carton by Jack Speck, Bindery Manager at the Country Press

Art book publishing

Above First monograph on Henry Moore, printed by Lund Humphries, 1934.
Opposite Carto(o)n by Jack Speck, Bindery Manager.

When the name Lund Humphries is mentioned nowadays, the immediate association is with art book publishing. Few know that this originated from a Bradford print works whose decision to start publishing art books was a major risk to take, and a major event in the publishing world, let alone in that of printing. What was novel about the decision was that these were not just to be books on any old art subject, but were to be monographs on contemporary artists, largely unknown, except to a small exquisite band of connoisseurs.

Although it is generally thought that Lund Humphries was a British pioneer in such a venture, it had, in fact, been tried before when the publisher Ernest Benn began, in 1923, to publish a series actually titled *Contemporary British Artists*. This seems to have been the brainchild of a youthful Victor Gollancz, working at Benn at that time. Curiously the series has a link to Bradford, and, indeed to Lund Humphries, for it was edited by a Bradford textile manufacturer's son, Albert Rutherston, whose brother, Charles, without intention, could be said to have started Lund Humphries on its path to becoming an art book publisher. Charles Rutherston, the son who stayed with the family firm, was an active member of the Bradford Arts Club, and built up an art collection of national importance. It was Charles who introduced Gregory to Henry Moore!

A further issue is, as to when Lund Humphries could claim to have entered the art book publishing field, for repeatedly, one researcher merely repeating what others wrote before, the date given is with the publication of *An Organic Architecture* in 1939. This had come about through Gregory's support, and indeed, publishing of an architecture magazine – *Focus*, edited by a lecturer at the Architectural Association, Anthony Cox. Cox had become involved in Frank Lloyd Wright's visit to London in that year, and in the series of lectures given by Wright at the Royal Institute of British Architects that were to attract a remarkably large audience. Such popular acclaim led to the decision to publish the lectures verbatim with Cox as co-editor and Lund Humphries the publisher and printer. On reflection this seems a one-off opportunist event rather than an initial step of a well-thought out policy decision. Eric and Gregory were shortly to be caught up in wartime activity – Eric, with his technical expertise on a secret mission at the Works related to the development of the atomic bomb, Gregory at the Ministry of Information; paper and print were severely rationed; hardly an opportune moment to launch a new venture.

In fact Lund Humphries' book publishing took an entirely different direction with Bruno Schindler, the sinologist, who was now responsible for overall publishing, and with the War Office in need of linguists, Lund Humphries consequently proceeded to issue a successful range of dictionaries and language teaching books.

When the company appears to have really shown its intent to publish art books the enterprise revolved around three Yorkshire men – Gregory, Henry Moore and Herbert Read (later to involve some of Read's neighbours in Hampstead – Ben Nicholson, Barbara Hepworth, Paul Nash and Naum Gabo). Gregory's introduction to Moore, in 1923, was not just a casual encounter, but one starting a lifelong friendship. Moore was to write –

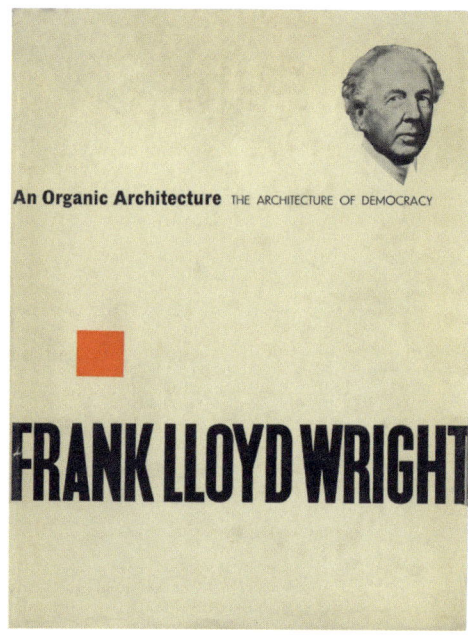

Above *An Organic Architecture* by Frank Lloyd Wright, 1939, published by Lund Humphries.

Art Book Publishing

> *'...an acquaintance that grew slowly into what was to be the closest friendship of my life, there are few men who have done as much, so modestly, for young living artists.'*

Gregory and Read had, prior to the war, in 1934, been involved in an early modest publication on Moore's work that came about under the aegis of Anton Zwemmer, the art bookshop and gallery owner. Moore, as were so many young artists, a frequenter of the bookshop where could be found the latest art books and journals from the Continent. Zwemmer and Moore conceived the idea of a small book on his work. Moore persuaded Gregory to extend credit to Zwemmer to cover printing costs, and Zwemmer to pay Read to write the text. The book did not sell well and Zwemmer is reported to have walked the streets of London trying to flog it.

It was in 1944 that the triumvirate – Read, Moore and Gregory, thought up the idea of an altogether more impressive volume – *Henry Moore; Sculpture and Drawings*, with an introduction by Read. This not only was to kick-start Lund Humphries as an art book publisher, laying the grounds for future editions, but gave the firm the confidence to proceed to publish monographs on other contemporary artists, and to continue with Moore (a project that was to build to a six volume catalogue raisonné).

Douglas Cooper, the art critic, wrote of the now returned Gregory's intent –

> *'To produce the best possible book, one which would do most honour to the artist and help to make his work better and more widely appreciated.'*

Above *Focus* no.3, 1939. Edited by Anthony Cox, published by Lund Humphries.

A pioneering printer

The first period of Lund Humphries' art book publishing has been described as belonging to Moore's friends, for, in the remaining years of the 1940s and into the 50s, the firm produced further monographs – on Barbara Hepworth, Ben Nicholson, and Naum Gabo. It also saw through the publication of one on Paul Nash writings, that Nash himself had begun to plan before his death in 1946; Read continued to contribute introductions.

This new activity proved to be something of a challenge to Lund Humphries printers with the likes of Moore wanting personal supervision of the photography of his works and Gabo's volume including ten works in three-dimensional colour, requiring special glasses to be seen clearly!

After Gregory's death in 1959, Anthony Bell, who succeeded him, was determined to carry on Gregory's intent. John Taylor, who had joined Lund Humphries from Macmillan's, became head of the publishing department, admitting, on his arrival, that he was fairly well ignorant of British contemporary art; he was to become quickly educated in the subject. Bell invited Alan Bowness to become the firm's editorial advisor, and he was to continue as such for some forty years, long after Lund Humphries had disposed of its art book publishing subsidiary.

It no doubt helped that Bowness was Hepworth's son-in-law, responsible for her estate, but he was to become key through his own reputation – lecturer at the Courtauld Institue, Director of the Tate Gallery, and Director of the Henry Moore Foundation. Bowness in the 1960s and 70s was to write and/or edit Lund Humphries monographs for a next generation of artists – William Scott, Alan Davie, Ivan Hitchens and Elizabeth Frink, along with an updated one on Hepworth.

When John Taylor is described as heading Lund Humphries

Above Roland Penrose, Henry Moore and Peter Gregory at the Venice Biennale, 1948.
Below John Taylor at the Zwemmer Gallery, 1978.

Above *Babara Hepworth 1960-69*, edited by Alan Bowness.

publishing department, this perhaps gives an inflated impression as the 'department' was rarely more than two people – Taylor and Charlotte Burri, although Spencer was still around in an advisory capacity. Taylor had met Burri at a Frankfurt Book Fair. At the time she was working for Phoebus Verlag and was extremely knowledgable about international co-edition publishing. Burri was eager to settle in London and, whilst Taylor was away on a trade mission in Canada he returned to find she had been taken on by his assistant, Mignon Alexandra, who was about to retire. It was Zwemmer who named Taylor and Burri, Herr Direcktor and Josephine.

Lund Humphries hived of its art book publishing arm as a subsidiary in 1969. Zwemmer became its distributer world-wide, replacing Alec Tiranti. And it was Zwemmer who was to purchase the subsidiary in 1976 when Lund Humphries was seeking funds to update its plant. In fact John Taylor had met Zwemmer's son, Desmond, when both were studying book and magazine publishing at the London College of Printing and they were to work amicably together when the publishing arm relocated from Bedford Square to what had been Zwemmer's gallery in Litchfield Street. As, soon after, the printers itself moved into Zwemmer's art bookshop it was, as John Taylor described it, 'confusing'.

That Lund Humphries Publishing, with various ups and downs and ownership, became one of the leading British publishers of books on art, architecture and design, along with Phaidon and Thames & Hudson, is another story, beyond its years as a venture of Lund Humphries, the Bradford printer.

A jobbing printer to the end

'The ten years from 1923 to 1933 take a high place in the history of printing renaissance. It was no red-hot revolution with a great body of printers experiencing some wonderful conversion. Indeed what was being done was being done by astonishingly few. The pioneers were out to show how modern methods and modern machinery could produce well-designed printing which was economical in cost could be counted on the fingers of both hands.'
Herbert Simon, of the Curwen Press, wrote of the printing industry after the First World War.

Although Lund Humphries was probably not the most economical, it could certainly claim one of the fingers, along with the likes of the Curwen Press, Cowell's of Ipswich, and the Baynard Press. Lund Humphries is now largely remembered for its show pieces – the Bedford Square open-door offices, *Penrose Annual*, *Typographica* and the monographs on contemporary artists – these overshadow the fact that it was one of the most outstanding jobbing printers of its day, not just able to cope with the pernickety demands of Moore, the exacting standards of Spencer, or Schindler's Chinese typeface, but handling the day-to-day needs of local and national clients.

Lubelski lists some dozen major companies, many international, across industries who, at one time or another, became clients, including

Above Zwemmer Gallery exhibition invitation designed by Maurice Bennett, for the Spanish artist Fransisco Borès. 1930s, a regular exhibitor in company with Picasso.
Opposite *Stitchcraft* magazine, printed by Lund Humphries, 1930s – 1960s.

Rolls Royce, I.C.I., and British Steel in the manufacturing sector; the National Westminster Bank and Bradford & Bingley Building Society in the financial; along with a number in the burgeoning media sector including Granada Television and Saatchi & Saatchi. And to these can be added many organisations related to the Arts, largely obtained from Bedford Square – museums and art galleries, such as the Victoria & Albert, the Tate and the National Gallery, major art auction houses as Sotheby's and Christie's, and, indeed, the Arts Council itself.

The company maintained its high standards whether it was handling a small privately published book on William Roberts' WWI experiences (of which a mere handful would be sold), knitting patterns for Paton & Baldwin, a thousand page pharmacopoeia, or a catalogue for a *Rebuilding Britain* exhibition at the National Gallery, that sold over 20,000 copies, or at the end of its existance, while the contents of the *Laura Ashley Home* catalogues were printed elsewhere, by web-offset lithography, the covers for each of the ten worldwide editions were printed by sheet-fed lithography by Lund Humphries in Bradford, having been designed in London by Trickett & Webb.

What was Lund Humphries offering that made it stand out from the rest? Beyond the basics of staying ahead of the field in its machinery and typefaces, were its standards. Its 1945 Works Handbook exemplifies its practice –

> '...every piece of printing and binding which is turned out by the Company shall be fine in design, typography and the excellence of its workmanship, both from the point of view of craftsmanship and technical accomplishment. All members should feel proud of the Company's product and wish to harness craftsmanship to the machine, so that although mass

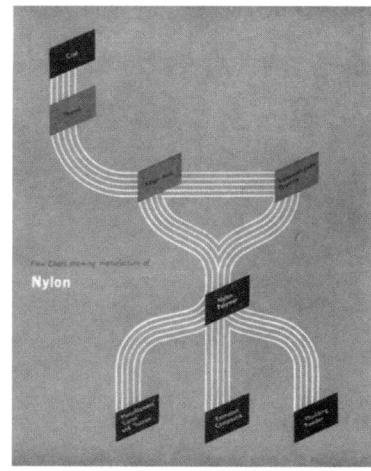

Above Brochure for Imperial Chemical Industries Ltd. (Plastics Division). Printed and designed by Lund Humphries

Above *4.5 Howitzer Gunner R.F.A. 1916–1918: Memories of the War to End War 1914–1918* by William Roberts.
Right Catalogue for the *Rebuilding Britain* exhibition at the National Gallery, 1943. Published for The Royal Institute of British Architects and printed by Lund Humphries.

A pioneering printer

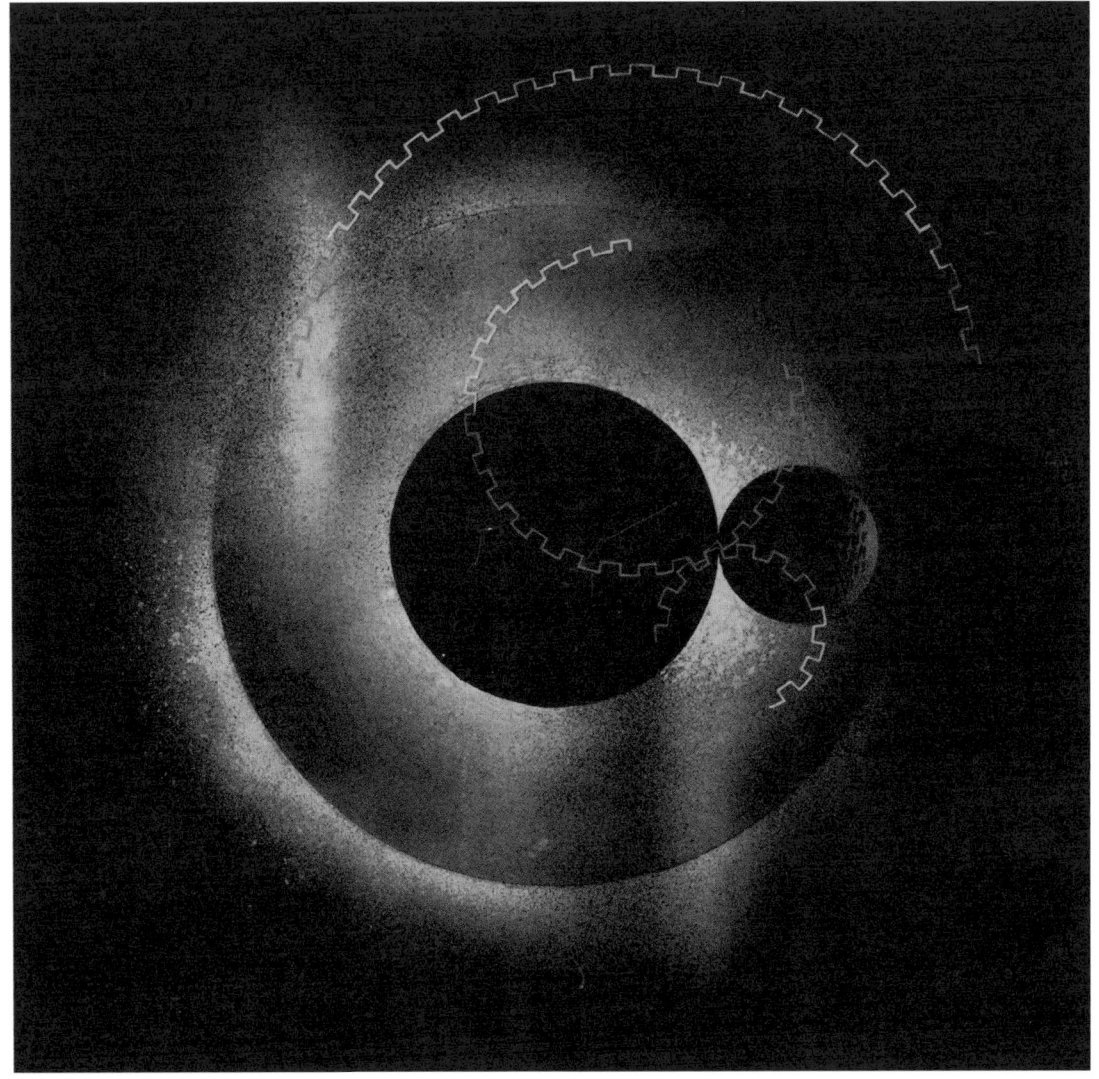

A jobbing printer to the end

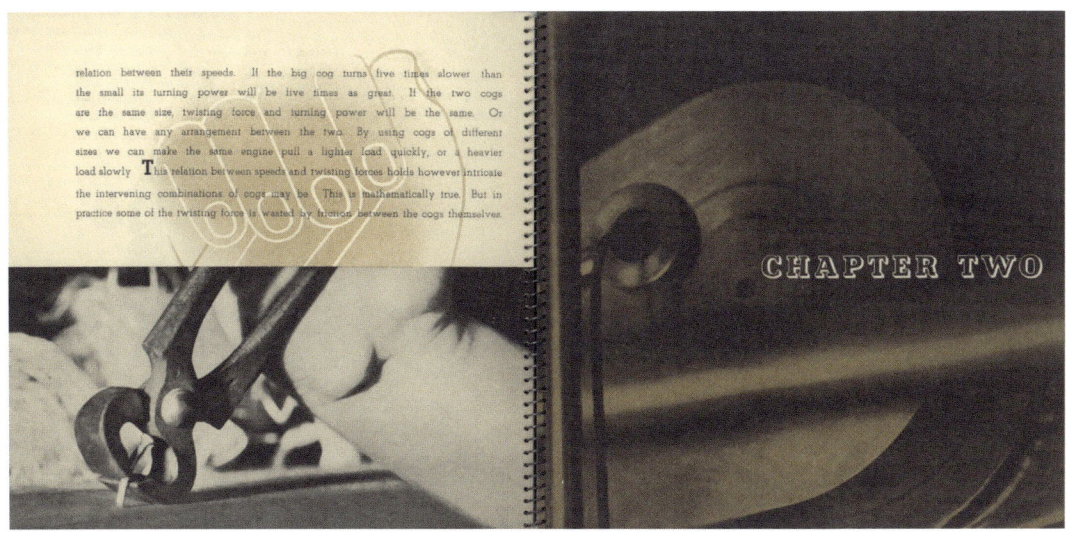

This Page The Self Changing or
Pre-Selective Epicyclic Gear, 1934.
Published by Shell Lubrication Oil.
Designed and illustrated by Zero
(Hans Schleger).

A pioneering printer

production may sometimes be involved, printing and binding may at the same time be created that is finely designed and executed and will raise the standard of work in this country.'

This statement has more than a whiff of evangelism about it. And so it was, for in addition to being among the pioneers technically and aesthetically, Lund Humphries had the fortune to have generations of exceptional managers and advisers, all with the mission to raise standards in the industry and to demonstrate that printing was part-and-part of graphic design; Anthony Bell described them as striving to be architects rather than plumbers of printing.

Percy Lund and Edward Humphries being succeeded by Peter Gregory and Eric Humphries, and then Anthony Bell and John Taylor, along with their outstanding art advisers – McKnight Kauffer, Herbert Spencer, and Alan Bowness – were a remarkable crew to be steering a printing company. They were largely modest men, lacking in self-importance, yet fiery when it came to crusading. And some might add that their missionary spirit was fuelled by their origins, for at least the managers, were Yorkshiremen, either born and bred or by adoption.

So where did it all go wrong? Sometimes quoted is an early company advertisement in a *Penrose Annual* –

'Devoted to the production of high-class printing, book-binding and the manufacturing of stationery, all of which is done a little better than seems necessary.'

Lubelski writes of the company remaining steadfast to the last in 'refusing to give way to the tawdry, the inferior and the mediocre', hitting the nail on the head with 'high quality comes at a price'. He

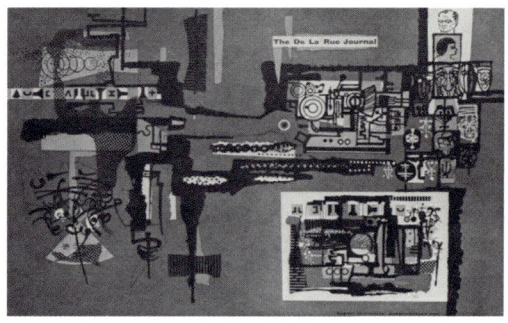

Above Illustration for *Benvenuto Cellini* by Eric Fraser. Printed by Lund Humphries, 1930s.
Below *De La Rue Journal*, the banknote printer's house magazine, designed by Alan Lindsay. Printed by Lund Humphries.

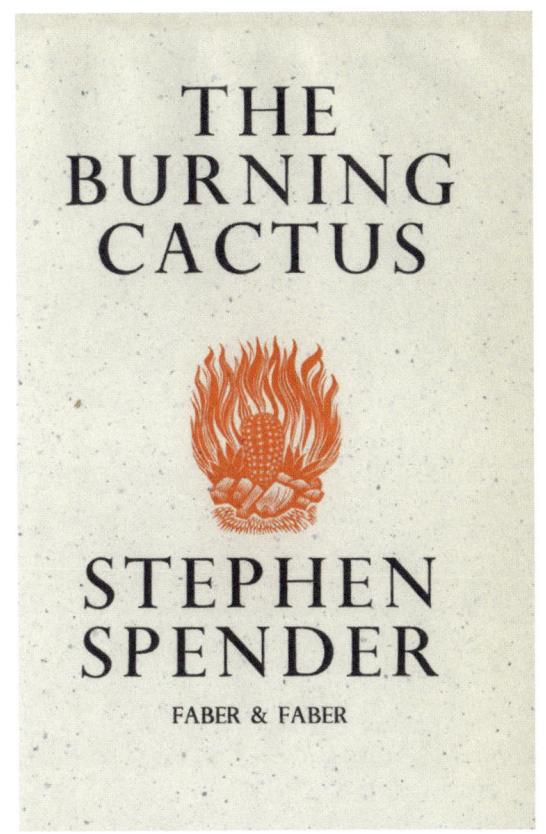 

Above Book jackets printed by Lund Humphries for Faber & Faber, 1930s.
Left Wood engraving by Reynolds Stone. *Right* Illustrated by Edward Bawden

SHEEPSKIN rugs to-day

CLARK, SON & MORLAND LTD. GLASTONBURY

A jobbing printer to the end

exemplifies this with the absurd amount of resources allocated to its client Patons & Baldwins, knitting wool manufacturers, with its monthly magazine *Stitchcraft*, when other clients would have proved more remunerative. The general conclusion seems to be that Lund Humphries might have survived if it had concentrated more on making profits than making perfect.

But Lund Humphries was not operating in a vacuum. The world was moving on, and moving on rapidly. Printing was only one of Britain's industries that went into decline in competition with overseas enterprises, with their non-unionised cheaper labour, and with decreasing transport costs. And technically the world was being revolutionized at a pace difficult for many companies to keep apace with, with craft having given way to machines and then to digitisation. Lund Humphries had already sold off its book publishing subsidiary to up-date its works in 1976. It was to fight the good fight for nearly another couple of decades before forced into liquidation in 1994.

It is perhaps paradoxical that it was the art book publishing, a very small part of its overall business activities, that it had eventually rejected, that was to keep the name Lund Humphries before the public, through changes of ownership, striving, as so many publishers nowadays, to survive in our digital internet dominated culture and now well-established overseas competition.

Above *Laura Ashley Home*, 1994. Textiles and home furnishings catalogue produced in ten worldwide editions. Designed by Trickett and Webb, covers printed by Lund Humphries.

Opposite Sheepskin Rugs Today, compiled by Humphrey Morland and Christopher Morland, published by Clark, Son & Morland. Designed and printed by Lund Humphries, 1930s.

Bibliography

The source book on Lund Humphries is Charles Lubelski's *Pride, Passion and Printing, the life and times of Percy Lund Humphries, The Country Press, Bradford*, printed in 2018. This gives comprehensive references not only for the company history, but for the 20th century British printing industry in its socio-economic context. Sources used for the chapter on *Penrose Annual* were the *Penrose Annuals* themselves; and for that on *Typographica*, Rick Poynor's *Typographica* published in 2001 by Laurence King Publishing. There are a few publications by Lund Humphries employees, largely no more than small booklets, but nevertheless illuminating –

1981   Anthony Bell   *Eye Witness of An Era – some memories of Lund Humphries in the 1930s*

1999   John Taylor   *Anecdotes of an art-book publisher, 40 years at Lund Humphries 1959-1999*

2015   ed. Lucy Myers   *Lund Humphries, celebrating 75 years of art book publishing 1939-2014*

Exhibitions at 12 Bedford Square

1933	*Francis Brugière and McKnight Kauffer*
1934	*Hans Schleger*
1934	*The Cresset Press*
1934	*An Exhibition of Commercial Design*
1934	*Man Ray*
1935	*McKnight Kauffer*
1935	*Rudolf Koch and the Kingspor Foundry*
1935	*Jan Tschichold*
1936	*An Exhibition of Printing & Commercial Design*
1937	*Lewitt Him*
1938	*Foreign Automobile Industry*
1938	*Three Australians*
1939	*Celebration of the 55th Anniversary of Percy Lund Humphries*
1952	*Purpose & Pleasure*
1963	*Typography in Britain Today*

Opposite and Right McKnight Kauffer's 'Mechanical Man' based on an artist's lay figure was designed for Shell-Mex and made an appearance in Hans Schleger's *Epicyclic Gears*, 1934.